GREGORY L. VOGT

VENUS

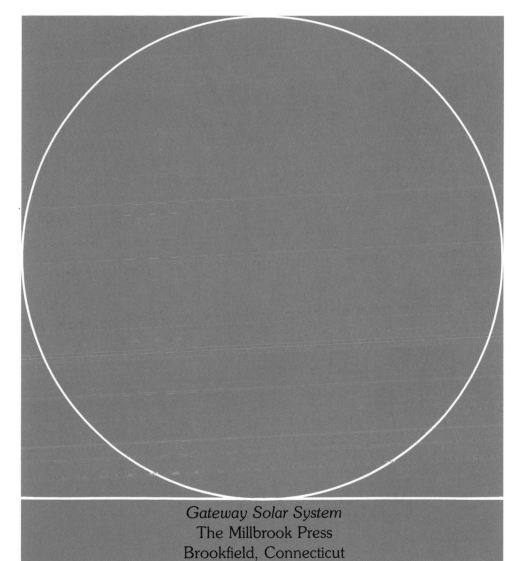

Gateway Solar System
The Millbrook Press
Brookfield, Connecticut

Published by The Millbrook Press
2 Old New Milford Road
Brookfield, Connecticut 06804

Library of Congress Cataloging-in-Publication Data

Vogt, Gregory.
Venus / by Gregory L. Vogt.
p. cm. — (Gateway solar system)
Includes bibliographical references and index.
Summary: Presents information on Venus, including its volcanoes,
arachnoids, and pancake domes, as studied by U.S. and Soviet
spacecraft. Includes a glossary and "Venus Quick Facts."
ISBN 1-56294-391-X (lib.bdg.)   ISBN 0-7613-0159-3 (pbk.)
1. Venus (Planet)—Juvenile literature.   2. Astronautics in
astronomy—Juvenile literature.   [1. Venus (Planet).] I. Title.
II. Series: Vogt, Gregory. Gateway solar system.
QB621.V643 1994
523.4'2—dc20   93-11217 CIP AC

Photographs and illustrations courtesy
National Aeronautics and Space Administration

Solar system diagram by Anne Canevari Green

VENUS

Thick clouds hide the surface of Venus in this photograph taken by the *Pioneer 10* spacecraft. An artist added stars to the picture.

More than 450 years ago, people had a strange idea about the universe. They believed the Earth was at its center and the sun, moon, planets, and all the stars revolved around it. Actually, the idea wasn't so strange. After all, the sun rose in the east and set in the west, and so did all the other objects in the heavens. What people didn't know was that the Earth was a planet spinning around on its *axis*—an imaginary line running from its north to its south pole. Like a moving carousel, Earth's spin made objects in the sky seem to fly past it.

Not everyone believed in an Earth-centered universe. One doubter was a Polish monk named Nicholas Copernicus. Copernicus studied the movements of the planets and stars and decided that it was really the Earth that was moving. Earth was spinning at the same time it was revolving around the sun. He couldn't prove that theory, but his idea made sense to an Italian astronomer who was born 21 years after Copernicus died. Galileo Galilei, the first astronomer to use a telescope to study the heavens, made a startling discovery.

Except for the sun and the moon, Venus is the brightest object in our sky. At times, however, it appears bigger and brighter than it does at other times. When Galileo looked at Venus with his telescope, he discovered the reason. The planet Venus had *phases*. Phases are changes in Venus's appearance. Sometimes, Venus was full, like a full moon. Months later, it would look like a half moon. Still later, Venus would show up as a thin crescent of light. When it was full, Venus was very small in Galileo's telescope. But when it was a crescent it was much larger.

Venus at half phase.

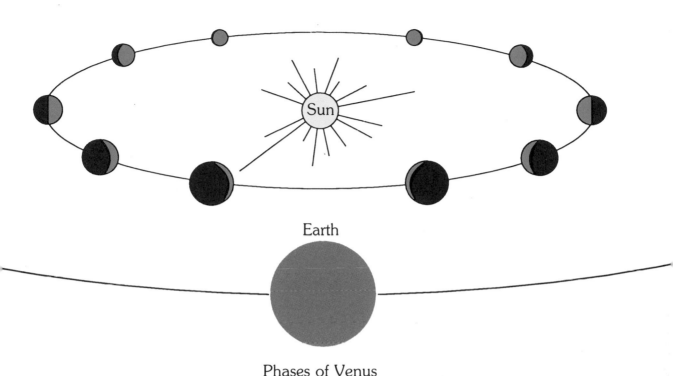

Earth

Phases of Venus

These observations meant two things to Galileo. First, instead of circling the Earth, Venus must be orbiting (traveling around) the sun. Second, Venus's *orbit* must be closer to the sun than the Earth's.

How did Galileo conclude this? He realized that, like our moon, planets don't give off their own light. Instead, they reflect sunlight. Through his telescope, he could see that when Venus appeared as a full circle, it looked small. Venus was on the far side of the sun, with its whole lighted side facing Earth. It looked small because it was far away. Then, when Venus was halfway around the sun, Galileo could see half its lighted side. The planet looked like a half moon. Finally, when Venus appeared as a thin crescent in Galileo's telescope, he knew that its dark side must be facing Earth. Venus was between Earth and the sun.

Knowing that Venus orbited the sun caused Galileo to question the other planets, too. Why shouldn't they orbit the sun as well? Galileo's discovery of the phases of Venus provided important evidence that Copernicus's theory was correct—the sun was at the center of the solar system.

The Second Planet

If you ever made a wish on a bright star, you probably wished on Venus. When it is visible in the evening sky, Venus is very bright. It is the first "star" to come out after the sun has set. At other times, Venus rises just before dawn and appears as a bright morning star.

With a telescope, an *astronomer* (a scientist who studies objects in outer space) can easily see the reason for Venus's brightness. Venus is covered by dense white clouds that reflect the sun's light strongly. In all the time since Galileo pointed his first telescope at Venus, no as-

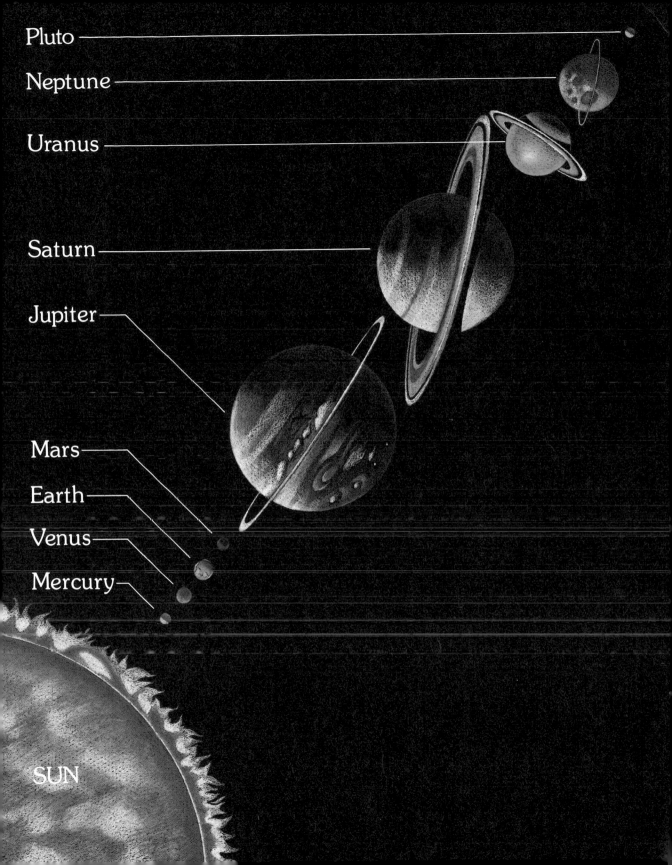

Pluto

Neptune

Uranus

Saturn

Jupiter

Mars

Earth

Venus

Mercury

SUN

If Venus's clouds were stripped away and it were placed next to Earth, the two planets might look like this. In this picture low areas are colored shades of blue. Higher areas are colored green, tan, and white.

tronomer has ever seen the surface of the planet. The clouds have never parted. But even with the clouds, astronomers have learned much about Venus.

Venus is the second planet out from the sun. It orbits the sun at a distance of 67 million miles (108 million kilometers) and takes 225 days to make a complete trip. Earth orbits the sun at a distance of 93 million miles (149.5 million kilometers). At the times when Venus's orbit takes it between Earth and the sun, Venus is less than 26 million miles (42 million kilometers) from Earth. This makes Venus Earth's closest neighbor in the solar system.

Venus is also nearly the same size as Earth. Its diameter of 7,521 miles (12,104 kilometers) is only a few hundred miles smaller than that of Earth. Because they are similar in size and their orbits are not far apart, many astronomers at first thought of Venus as Earth's twin.

What must the surface of Venus be like? For years, astronomers could only guess. Because it is closer to the sun and has dense clouds, they reasoned that Venus must be very hot. Clouds would trap some of the sun's energy and raise Venus's temperature much the same way a greenhouse on Earth traps the sun's energy and gets hot. Venus might, they thought, be covered with a steamy jungle of lush green plants. It might be a desert world, or it might be covered with oceans of water or petroleum.

The First Spacecraft Arrives

There were many theories about the surface of Venus, but astronomers lacked solid data. Then, in the 1950s, astronomers began to use new techniques to learn about Venus. With *radio telescopes* that capture radio waves from space, they confirmed that Venus is very hot. A few years later, in 1962, the first successful interplanetary spacecraft flew past Venus. The spacecraft, *Mariner 2,* was launched by the National Aeronautics and Space Administration (NASA). *Mariner 2* passed within about 21,000 miles (34,000 kilometers) of Venus's cloudtops. As it zipped past the planet, it took Venus's temperature and measured its atmosphere. Data showed that Venus's surface is hot enough to melt zinc—900 degrees Fahrenheit (482 degrees Celsius). Such high temperatures meant that Venus had no jungles or oceans. Plants would burn up, and oceans would evaporate. Venus had to have a hard, rocky surface.

Mariner 2 also discovered that the atmosphere of Venus is made up mostly of carbon dioxide gas (the gas

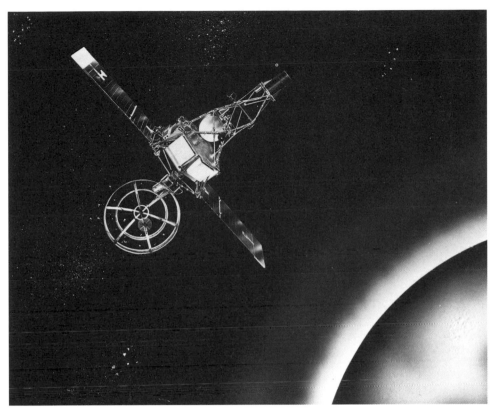

The first successful interplanetary spacecraft, *Mariner 2*, flew past Venus in 1962.

you expel when you breathe). The pressure of the gas is 90 times greater at the surface of Venus than the pressure of air at the surface of the Earth.

Many other spacecraft were sent to Venus. Some were launched by NASA and some by the Soviet Union. There were orbiting spacecraft, probes that measured the

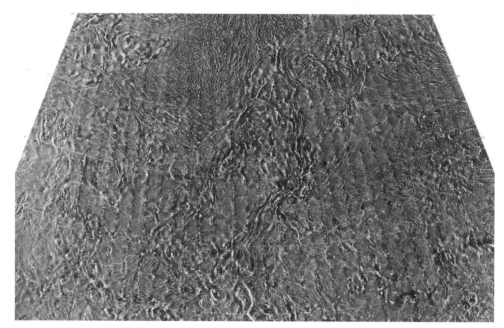

The *Venera* spacecraft, launched by the Soviet Union, used radar to create pictures of Venus's surface.

atmosphere as they fell through it, lander craft, and even balloons that drifted about in Venus's atmosphere while dangling scientific instruments beneath them. Astronomers also used large radar antennas on Earth to send powerful radar waves to Venus. The waves penetrated Venus's clouds and bounced off its hard surface. When the waves returned to Earth, astronomers were able to construct crude maps of high and low spots on Venus. By repeatedly sending the radar waves to Venus, they observed that these spots moved. That meant that Venus was rotating (spinning) on its axis. But the *rotation rate* was very slow—Venus took 243 days to spin once on its axis. Radar also showed that Venus rotates in the opposite direction from Earth. On Venus, the sun rises in the west and sets in the east. Venus's opposite rotation and slow spin make its day longer than its year!

A Nasty Place

It is unlikely that people will ever set foot on Venus to explore its surface. Venus has fatally high temperatures and pressures at its surface and an atmosphere made of carbon dioxide, which is poisonous. To make things worse, the dense clouds of Venus are made of a fog of sulfuric acid.

Even without the benefit of human exploration, we have a pretty good idea about what the surface of Venus looks like, thanks to four spacecraft. All four orbited the planet and used radar to penetrate the clouds and map the land below. In this mapping technique, radar waves are sent to the surface and bounce back. Waves that bounce off high objects, like mountains, return to the spacecraft first. Waves bouncing off lower objects, like deep valleys, take longer to come back. The waves' different arrival times tell how high the surface is at every

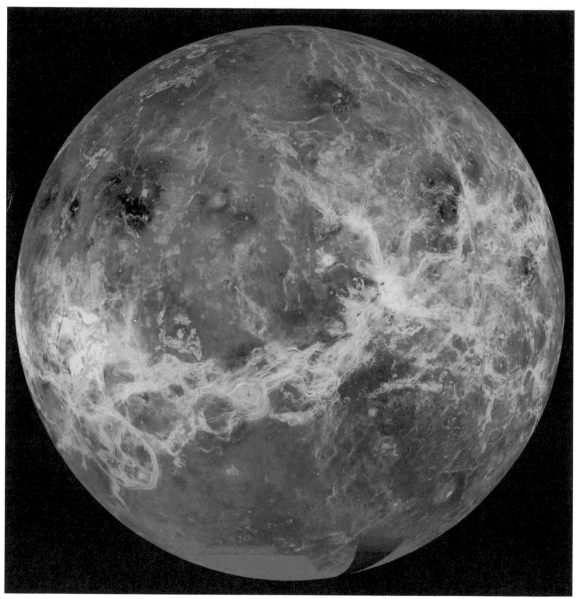

A computer-generated picture shows Venus as it might look without its clouds. The bright band near the middle of the planet is *Aphrodite Terra,* a region about the size of Africa. The orange colors are based on colors seen by unmanned Soviet spacecraft that landed on Venus.

point beneath the spacecraft. The spacecraft then converts that information to a long stream of computer numbers that are radioed to Earth. Computers on Earth process the numbers into pictures and maps of the surface.

The four spacecraft that gave us pictures and maps are *Venera 15* and *16,* launched by the Soviet Union, and NASA's *Pioneer 10* and *Magellan.* Of the four

NASA's *Magellan* spacecraft, about to be launched from the space shuttle in 1989.

spacecraft, *Magellan* was the most recent and had the best radar system. It arrived at Venus in 1990 and made the most detailed survey of Venus's surface yet.

Today, we know that Venus's surface is very rugged. More than half of the planet is covered with rolling plains. About one quarter is covered with lowlands, and the rest is highlands.

A Volcanic World

When mountains are formed on Earth, they are immediately attacked by the forces of *erosion*. Wind, running water, and ice wear down the rock and smooth its surface. Over hundreds of millions of years, entire mountain ranges can be wiped away, making it difficult to learn the history of a region. On Venus, erosion is much slower. Venus's thick atmosphere is very sluggish. It blows across the surface at a speed of only about 3 miles (5 kilometers) per hour or less. And the planet is too hot to have rain and ice to wear away the land. Therefore, mountains and valleys on Venus remain sharp and easy to study even half a billion years after they formed. This makes Venus a scientist's paradise.

We know today that Venus is a volcanic world. Scientists studying *Magellan* radar images have identified

Maat Mons is a volcano 5 miles (8 km) high. Around it, lava flows extend for hundreds of miles across cracked plains. This computer-generated picture is based on radar data collected by *Magellan*.

430 large volcanoes, each 12 miles (20 kilometers) wide or larger, and tens of thousands of smaller ones. More than 80 percent of Venus is covered by lava flows. Much of the volcanic activity on Venus seems to have taken place about 500 million years ago. Scientists have estimated this age by the number of *craters* found on the surface. When a *comet* or *asteroid* smacks into a planet or a moon, it blasts out a crater, or big hole. The debris

from the collision piles up around the outside of the crater, and there is often a small mountain peak left in its middle.

Studies of Earth's moon and Mercury have shown that the inner solar system—the region between Earth and the sun—has been peppered with asteroid and comet impacts. Mercury and the moon have thousands of cra-

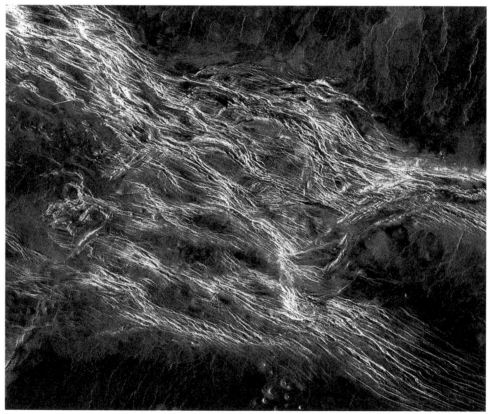

Radar images from *Magellan* show sharp ridges and wrinkles in Venus's surface.

ters each. Earth would, too, if erosion had not wiped away their traces. So far, scientists have identified only about 800 craters on Venus, and they are all fairly recent (in planetary time, that is). Since there should be many more craters, something must have wiped them away. That something was the planet-wide lava flows that took place 500 million years ago.

Arachnoids, Pancakes, and Splotches

Venus is a world that is difficult to describe in a few words. *Magellan* pictures have shown that Venus is crisscrossed by cracks, flooded with hardened lava, poked open from the inside by thousands of volcanoes (one higher than Mount Everest on Earth), and blasted by asteroids and comets. The hard surface of Venus shows signs that it has been twisted, pulled, and compressed. Similar forces on Earth cause earthquakes, thrust up high mountain chains, and unleash volcanoes. Those forces on Venus have broken the planet's crust, making it resemble a shattered automobile windshield.

In the midst of all this chaos are many strange surface markings. Perhaps the strangest are the *arachnoids*, so named because they look like the webs of spiders (arachnids). Some of these circular features are more

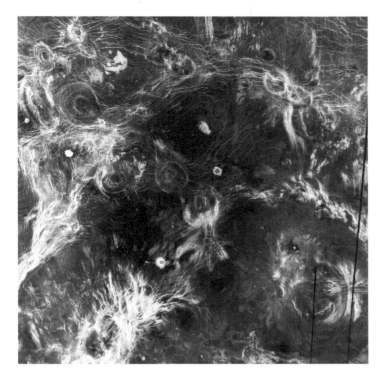

Weblike arachnoid fractures spread out in this *Magellan* radar picture.

than 100 miles (160 kilometers) across, although many are smaller. Near their centers are circular cracks, and stretching out from them—like the spokes of a bicycle wheel—are hundreds of cracks. Scientists think the arachnoids formed when molten rock accumulated just beneath the surface, causing the surface rock to bulge and fracture. When the molten rock cooled, it shrank, and the centers of the arachnoids collapsed into a maze of circular fractures.

Also strange are the *pancake domes*. These are flat-topped, steep-sided volcanic cones. Seen from above,

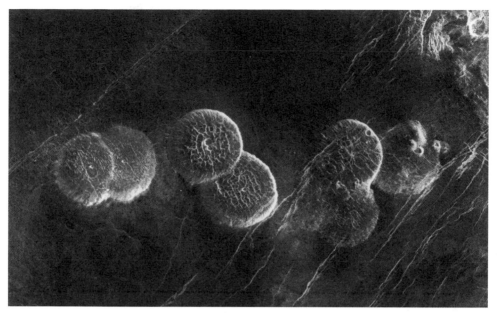
Volcanic pancake domes dot this *Magellan* picture. The domes rise as much as 2,460 feet (750 m) above broad lava plains.

they look like pancakes on a griddle. They were created by sticky lava oozing out from Venus's crust. The lava cooled as it spread out in a circular pattern. Most pancake domes are a few thousand feet high. Similar volcanic cones have formed on Earth, but they are quickly covered with plants and eroded by running water. Pancake domes on Venus have kept their shape for millions of years.

Although erosion on Venus is much slower than it is on Earth, it does take place. Flowing hot lava can widen cracks and smooth out plains, and asteroid and comet impacts can blast apart the surface. Unlike Earth and the moon, meteor impacts do not occur on Venus's surface. *Meteors,* chunks of space rock and metal, do slam into the planet, but friction with the dense atmosphere destroys them before they reach the surface.

Comets and asteroids, much larger than meteors, have a better chance of surviving the atmosphere. When they do, they blast out circular holes and scatter debris for hundreds of miles. However, sometimes even comets and asteroids don't make it all the way to the surface

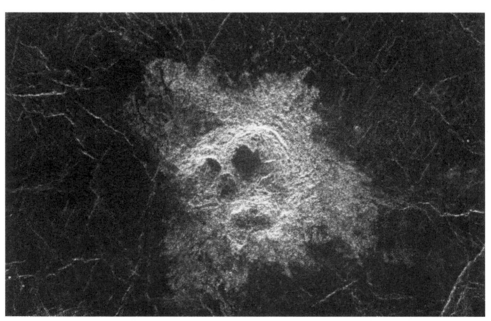

This crater cluster was made by a large meteor that broke up in Venus's thick atmosphere. Four chunks of the meteor blasted out overlapping craters and splashed rock and dust around them.

of Venus. A few have exploded in the atmosphere, and the shock waves have jumbled up the surface without creating craters. Scientists call these craterless impacts *splotches*.

A Dim Future?

Some people complain that we shouldn't waste our time studying other worlds when we have so many problems to solve on Earth. One of the biggest problems we face is pollution. Scientists are very worried that pollution is changing our atmosphere. For example, carbon dioxide is released by burning such things as coal, gasoline, and natural gas. How much carbon dioxide can we release in our atmosphere before it becomes a "greenhouse" and heats up? Will it become too hot to live on Earth someday?

Surprisingly, the answers to those questions and many others may not be found on Earth. They may be found on Venus. We know that Venus has lots of carbon dioxide in its atmosphere and that it is extremely hot. If scientists can find out how Venus became this way, they may learn how to prevent the same thing from happening to Earth. By studying Venus, Earth's "twin" in space, we can learn about our own world as well.

This computer-generated, false-color *Magellan* picture shows a bird's-eye view of an unnamed volcano on Venus. Scientists still have much to learn about Earth's "twin" planet.

VENUS QUICK FACTS

Venus: Named after the ancient Roman goddess of love and beauty.

	Venus	Earth
Average Distance from the Sun		
Millions of miles	67	93
Millions of kilometers	108	149.6
Revolution (one orbit around the sun)	225 days (0.62 Earth year)	365 days (1 year)
Average Orbital Speed		
Miles per second	22	18.6
Kilometers per second	35	30
Rotation (spinning once)	243 days	24 hours
Diameter at Equator		
Miles	7,521	7,926
Kilometers	12,104	12,756
Surface Gravity (compared to Earth's)	0.9	1
Mass (the amount of matter contained in Venus, compared to Earth)	0.82	1
Atmosphere	carbon dioxide	nitrogen, oxygen
Satellites (moons)	0	1

GLOSSARY

Arachnoids	Spiderweb-like fractures in the crust of Venus caused by molten rock squeezing under surface rock, then cooling and shrinking.
Asteroids	Chunks of rock up to a few hundred miles across that orbit the sun.
Astronomer	A scientist who studies planets, moons, stars, and other objects in outer space.
Axis	An imaginary line running through a planet from its north pole to its south pole.
Comet	Large chunks of ice and rock that orbit the sun and stream off gas tails when heated.
Erosion	Wearing away of land surface by the forces of flowing wind, water, and ice.
Magellan	NASA spacecraft that orbited Venus beginning in 1990 to make radar pictures and maps of the planet.
Mariner 2	The first successful interplanetary spacecraft that collected data about Venus as it flew by the planet in 1962.
Meteor	A piece of rock or metal that orbits the sun and sometimes collides with a planet or moon, burning up in its atmosphere or blasting out a crater on the surface.
Orbit	The path a planet takes to travel around the sun, or a moon to travel around a planet. (Also applies to the path a spacecraft follows when orbiting a planet.)
Pancake domes	Broad volcanic cones found on Venus.

Phases	Changes in the appearance of the moon, Mercury, and Venus because of the way sunlight falls on them.
Pioneer 10	Radar-mapping spacecraft that orbited Venus in 1978.
Radio telescope	Telescope that captures and concentrates radio waves from space.
Revolution	One complete orbit of a planet around the sun, or a moon around a planet.
Rotation	The spinning of a planet or moon around its axis.
Splotches	Craterless impacts on Venus caused when comets or asteroids explode in the planet's atmosphere just above the surface.
Venera 15 and *16*	Radar-mapping spacecraft sent to Venus by the Soviet Union.

FOR FURTHER READING

Asimov, I. *Isaac Asimov's Library of the Universe. Venus: A Shrouded Mystery.* Milwaukee, Wis.: Gareth Stevens Publishing, 1990.

Asimov, I. *Venus, Near Neighbor of the Sun.* New York: Lothrop, Lee & Shepard Books, 1981.

Brewer, D. *Planet Guides: Venus.* New York: Marshall Cavendish, 1992.

Gallant, R. *National Geographic Picture Atlas of Our Universe.* Washington, D.C.: National Geographic Society, 1980.

Rathburn, E. *Exploring Your Solar System.* Washington, D.C.: National Geographic Society, 1989.

Schloss, M. *Venus.* New York: Franklin Watts, 1991.

Vogt, G. *Magellan and the Radar Mapping of Venus.* Brookfield, Conn.: The Millbrook Press, 1992.

INDEX

Page numbers in *italics* refer to illustrations.

ABOUT THE AUTHOR

Gregory L. Vogt works for NASA's Education Division at the Johnson Space Center in Houston, Texas. He works with astronauts in developing educational videos for schools.

Mr. Vogt previously served as executive director of the Discovery World Museum of Science, Economics, and Technology in Milwaukee, Wisconsin, and was an eighth-grade science teacher. He holds bachelor's and master's degrees in science from the University of Wisconsin at Milwaukee, as well as a doctorate in curriculum and instruction from Oklahoma State University.